To:

From:

To my beloved grandchildren, Angelia,
William and Jeffrey whom I cherish.
— Sylvia C. Browne

Browne, Sylvia.
  Light a candle / by Sylvia Browne ;
edited by Kat Shehata ; design by Jo McElwee
p.cm.
ISBN 0-9717843-6-1

  1.Candles--Miscellanea. 2. Spiritual life--
Meditations. 3. Spiritual life--Miscellanea.
I. Title.

BF1442.C35B76 2006   133'.2
                           QB105-200166

Angel Bea Publishing
www.angelbea.com

Light a Candle

SYLVIA BROWNE

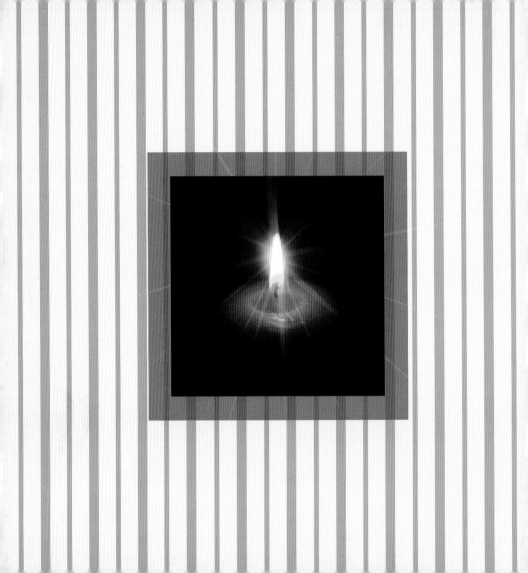

Dearest Friends,

As you read this book, light a candle. Say aloud or in your mind the affirmations, prayers, and positive thoughts on the following pages. Make a commitment to yourself to improve your life by raising your level of spiritual consciousness.

I was inspired to write this book because I have personally benefited from the spiritual energy of candles. No matter what it is you want to accomplish — better health, to find a new career, to connect with the spirits of loved ones, or protection and happiness for your family — you have the power within to make your dreams come true.

Use this book as a guide to help you create your own daily spiritual exercises. By taking time to concentrate on what is important in your life, you will increase your spirituality and become more proactive, and your aura of positive energy will shine and spread to those around you.

—Sylvia C. Browne

Light a Candle

For protection, love, prosperity, or in the memory of loved ones who have passed. Each time you light a candle with love in your heart, you increase your love of God, your self-awareness, and your spirituality.

For centuries, people around the world have burned candles in ceremonies, in religious rituals, during celebrations, and in remembrance of loved ones who have passed.

It is a universal truth that candles represent unity, peace, love, and spirituality.

Harness the positive energy of candles.

Affirmations

Affirmations are powerful
spiritual tools we can use
to achieve our goals in life.

Think of affirmations as
"positive thinking exercises."

Believe in yourself and know
that there is no such thing as
"impossible."

Empowerment

For nine nights, at precisely 9:00, light a candle and repeat this affirmation:

"As a blessed child of God, I am empowered to create miracles.

I have the power to make positive changes in my life. I will take the first step today by...

I have the power and strength to achieve my worthiest goals. Today I will begin my path to success by...

I am grateful for my life. I am especially thankful for...

The greatest gift I can give God is to help his children. Today I will help others by...

My family, friends, and pets mean everything to me. Dear Lord, I ask that you surround my loved ones in the white light of Your Holy Spirit. I ask protection for...

The white light
is God's sacred aura.

God shares His blessed light,
filled with infinite love, wisdom,
compassion, and power,
whenever we need it.

All we need to do to receive
God's gift is simply ask.

Believe in miracles and the
power of prayer.

Whether you believe in God
or not, He believes in you.

"Surround me with the white light of Your Holy Spirit"

Romance

Pray for love to come into your life, for love to last, and for yourself, that you are loving to those around you.

Light floating candles and burn rose-scented candles to create a romantic atmosphere.

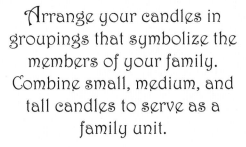

Family

Arrange your candles in groupings that symbolize the members of your family. Combine small, medium, and tall candles to serve as a family unit.

Light these candles and see their energy come together to form one unified glowing light.

Take this image of light and surround your family in this protective bubble. Ask God to keep your loved ones safe in His holy aura of white light.

Candles in clusters are symbolic of your friends and loved ones all burning together in tandem, all giving out light not only to each other, but to all who see and feel the energy.

Today I will shine like a candle that not only lights the darkness, but also brings joy and laughter to all who share my light.

The color, energy, and scent of candles can have multiple meanings.

Burn your candles,
feel the energy,
and decide what each
one means to you.

Arrange your candles as
you like. Assign energy to them.

When you light these candles,
pray for the people or
goals each one represents.

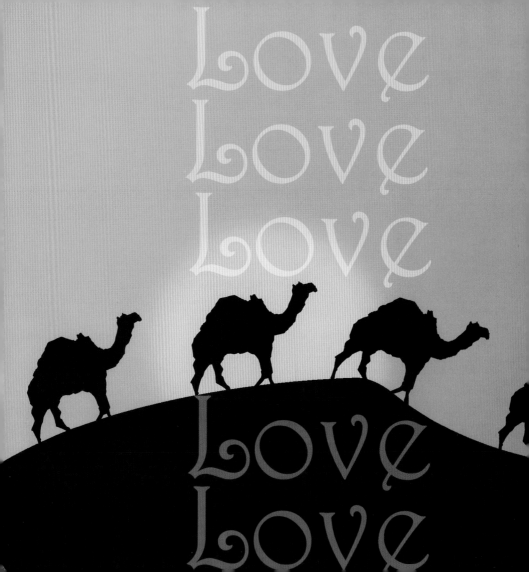

Dearest God,

Surround my family with Your blessed love. Let our loyalty to each other become stronger, not weaker, as we weather the seasons of our lives.

Harmony

Let the world understand that we must
use our natural resources wisely, so that
people, animals and nature can all exist
harmoniously in the circle of life.

Protect the earth and all You have given us.
Help us to care for the world and not to
pollute or hurt animals, nature, the elderly, and
all the people of the world. In times of peace
let the world rejoice. In times of hardship, let
people band together so that we may raise our
collective consciousness, dear Lord, to save
the earth and all that reside here.

Light a white candle for
Peace on Earth.

Dear God,
Keep your mantle of protection around all my dear pets. Bless my home with the presence of animal spirits and totems. Let the strength, courage, and loyalty of animals reflect on me and allow my spirit to mirror their souls' perfection.

If you have ever suffered the loss of a pet, I want you to know you are not alone. Unfortunately, there is no way to avoid the pain of losing a beloved family member. Please take comfort, though, and even joy, that all animals live happily forever on the Other Side. They frolic and play while they wait for us. In fact, they are so excited to see us when we come over that they push everyone else out of the way to be first in line to welcome us Home.

Protection for Pets

Light a Candle

Light a **jasmine-scented** candle to raise your spiritual consciousness.

Say a Prayer

Dearest God,
When I light this candle show
me the road to take to fulfill my
goals, not only for my learning,
but also for my higher purpose.

Tall candles reaching to the sky are messages to God.

Tall candles are also petitions and affirmations of spirituality. Light each candle one by one. Assign a message to each candle, say a prayer, and surround yourself with the white light of the Holy Spirit.

Light a Candle

Ask God, angels,

and your guides

to help you

achieve

your

dreams.

Be specific down to the tiniest detail.

 Program your mind for success.

 See yourself achieving your goals.

What are your goals?

What can you do right now to take the first step towards your success?

What
do you want
out of life?

Healing
Financial success
Spiritual awareness
Better Health
To start a family
A new career
Love
A new house
Protection
Longevity
Guidance
Peace

Focus on one goal at a time.
Do one thing every day that will
help you achieve your dreams.

Wisdom

Light a gold candle for
higher consciousness,
knowledge,
and wisdom.

Unravel the mysteries of life and pierce the veil of ignorance.

Past Memories

Black and white candles represent our past experiences. Light these candles and release painful memories.

Today is a new day. I am not afraid, burdened, or sad about the past. I will create joyful memories today and fill my spirit with happiness. My aura will reflect positive energy for all to see.

The past is behind me. I have learned from every positive and negative event in my life. I am stronger and wiser because of these experiences.

Light a green or pine-scented candle
for good health and spiritual well-being.

Dearest God, angels, and guides,
If I must be sick, let my symptoms be mild
and last only a short time. Let any and all
physical or mental pain be equivalent to a
"fender-bender" instead of a major crash.

For every challenge or setback we face in
life, our spirits have the ability to emerge
triumphant and stronger than before.

Whatever doesn't kill us
makes us stronger.

Balance

I can balance my responsibilities at work, at home and in my personal life. My world is full of duties and pleasures. I can find a healthy balance so that I am grateful for an active life, instead of resentful of my commitments.

Aura

Give the power of your own positive
energy to those blocked by negativity.

Have you ever known a person to walk
in and light up a room? Or perhaps you
have seen someone who has the opposite
effect. This is true because we all have an
aura of light around us that reflects our
attitudes. Some people have a positive
aura while others give off negative vibes.

Let my aura reflect gratitude, loyalty, and
commitment to myself, those around me,
and my Creator.

Attitudes are contagious

Share your Light

Can you make someone smile today?

Give a compliment to a co-worker?

Make someone laugh who is down?

Hug someone you love and tell them they are important in your life?

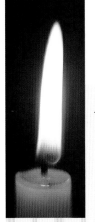

Let my positive spiritual energy shine so brightly that the darkness of negativity will never occupy my spirit.

My aura will radiate the white light of the Holy Spirit to all those I come in contact with at work, at home, and throughout my travels.

Energy

Let this be a symbol
of the lighthouse to
your soul.

It is important to light
a candle because our
loved ones, angels,
and guides can see a
burning light.

Feel the embrace of loved ones

Candles
truly are burning
positive energy.

Candles alone have no power.
The power of candles comes from
your own energy.

Light a candle.
Ask the spirits of your loved ones
to come to you. Close your eyes
and feel the warm embrace of their
eternal love.

The energy of your loved ones is
always with you. Feel their warmth,
talk to them, and know that you are
never alone. You are always loved.

Ask for a sign:

A bird in your window in the morning,
an unexpected call from a family member
"just because," or a special song on the
radio you haven't heard in a long time.

Keep my angels always near me.

Let me be aware of their presence and the whisper of their holy wings of protection.

Call Upon Angels

In your name, dearest God, send Angels with me everywhere I go. When I am sick, I pray to be touched by the healing scepter of the Archangels. Send Cherubim and Seraphim angels to lift my spirits with the heavenly sounds of their sweet music. When I need a miracle, send Powers to surround me with their holy wings of protection. Send Carrions to keep the earth safe from dark spirits and negative energy.

Keep my life on track with the aid of Virtues. For my higher learning, let my actions, both good and bad, be recorded by Dominions. Help me combat negativity by surrounding my spirit with an army of Thrones. When I am in immediate danger, I call upon Principalities to come to my rescue. When my faith is tested, when I need to know that everything in life happens for a reason, when I want to feel a connection to my eternal home, I ask for you, dear Lord, to surround my spirit with the blessed light of Your Holy Spirit.

Light three white
candles.

Connect

with your spirit guides

Ask your guides to follow the energy of the flame and come to your side.

In your mind or aloud, talk to your guides. Tell them about your goals and problems, or ask them for guidance.

The answers may come to you right away or they may come to you in dreams. You may also get information just "out of the blue" when you least expect it.

Listen...

Eternal Life

For most of us, in this lifetime or any other, the most difficult moments of our lives stem from the loss of a family member.

Let me tell you, without a shadow of doubt, our family members, animals, and the beauty and comfort of the earth are all waiting for us on the Other Side.

When our life on earth is over, a beautiful white tunnel will emerge from our own bodies.
Angels will come to guide us Home.

As we ascend through the tunnel, we will see our spirit guides, loved ones, and all of our dear pets.
Our eternal knowledge will return to us. We will remember that everything we experienced in life happened for a reason: our higher learning.

We will feel unconditional love, joy, and self-worth for all eternity.

About the Author

Millions of people have witnessed
Sylvia Browne's incredible psychic
powers on TV shows such as *Montel,
Larry King Live*, *Entertainment Tonight,*
and *Unsolved Mysteries*. Sylvia is the
author of numerous books and audios,
and has recently launched her own
merchandise line, The Sylvia Browne

Collection. She is also the president of the Sylvia Browne
Corporation and the founder of her church, the Society of
Novus Spiritus.

To learn more about Sylvia Browne and to see a schedule of
her TV and radio appearances and live shows, and her brand
new merchandise collection, log on to www.sylvia.org.

Sylvia Browne is coming to a city near you! If you enjoy
Sylvia's books and look forward to seeing her on TV, then
you will love seeing her in person. For more information
visit www.sylvia.org.

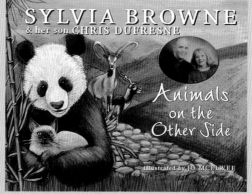

Peace

Surround me with
the white light of Your
Holy Spirit. Let me
shine like a candle,
that not only lights
the darkness, but also
brings peace & joy to
all that see and feel
my energy.
— Sylvia C. Browne

The
Sylvia Browne
Collection

www.sylvia.org
www.angelbea.com